Fun Zone

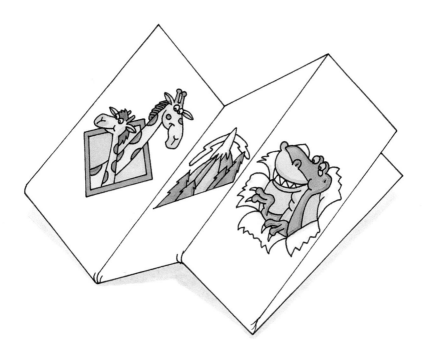

Written by Jo Windsor
Illustrated by Kelvin Hawley

Fun Zone

What is Fun Zone?

Fun Zone is a fun park. People come from all over the world for a fun time out. The park has six different fun places to visit.

People can ride the monorail train to Fun Zone from Freetown.

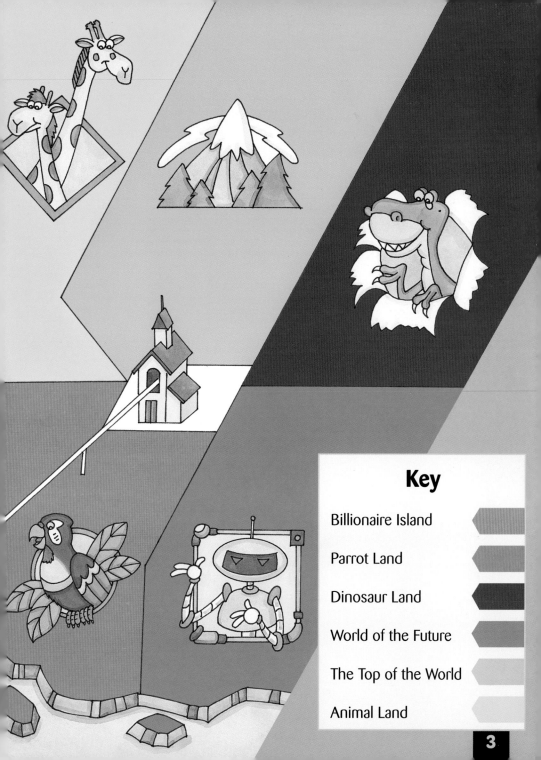

Key

Billionaire Island

Parrot Land

Dinosaur Land

World of the Future

The Top of the World

Animal Land

Billionaire Island

Things to do and see

- Visit Billionaire Beach – where billionaires have breakfast.
- Ride the cable car across the island.
- Walk the Lookout Track. (Watch out for traps!)
- Visit Cape Bay – where billionaires jetski.

Billionaire Island is home to many billionaires. People come to see how the billionaires live.

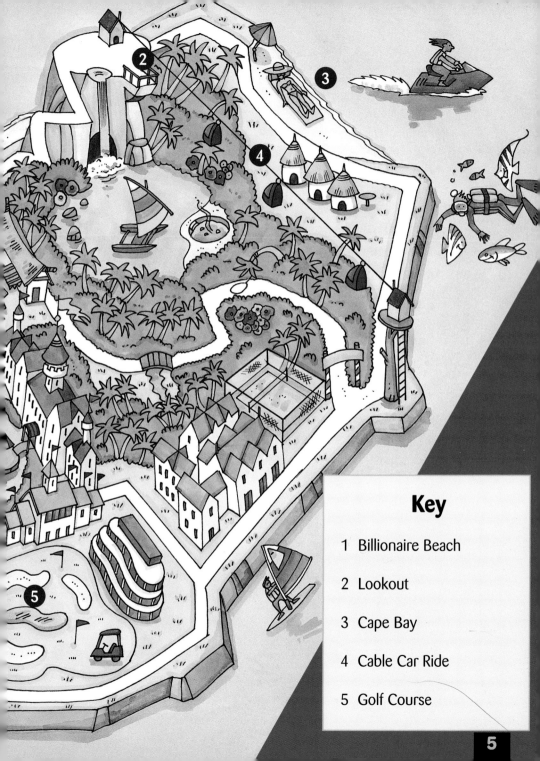

Key

1 Billionaire Beach

2 Lookout

3 Cape Bay

4 Cable Car Ride

5 Golf Course

Parrot Land

Things to do and see

- Visit the Parrot Pools – where parrots play on hot days.
- Visit the Parrot Play Centre – where young parrots have some fun.
- Visit "Talk School" – where parrots learn to talk.

Parrot Land has all kinds of parrots. There are walking tracks and lookouts for people who want to look closely at the birds.

Key

1. Lookouts
2. Talk School
3. Egg Nursery
4. Parrot Pools
5. Parrot Play Centre

---- Walking Track

Dinosaur Land

Things to do and see

- Ride the Monorail.
- Take a Hot Air Balloon Ride.
- Go on a Buggy Ride to see dinosaurs close up.
- Visit a Dinosaur Dig.

Dinosaur Land is a place of caves and volcanoes where dinosaurs live. The land has exciting things to do.

Key

	Monorail
	Hot Air Balloon Ride
	Volcanoes
	Mud Pools
	Dinosaur Dig
	Buggy Ride Track

World of the Future

Things to do and see

- See the house of the future.
- See the restaurant of the future.
- See Dome City.
- Meet the robot teachers at the robot school.

The **World of the Future** is a place where people work and live in a different way. You can ride through this world on jet buggies.

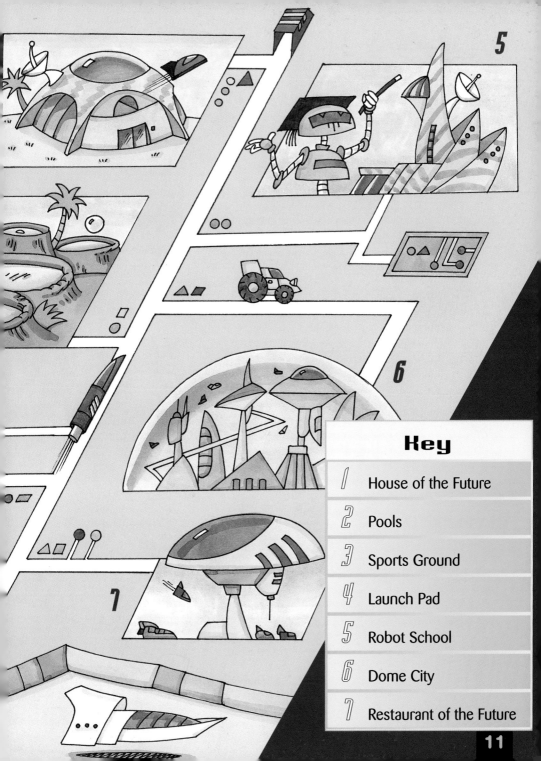

Key

1	House of the Future
2	Pools
3	Sports Ground
4	Launch Pad
5	Robot School
6	Dome City
7	Restaurant of the Future

The Top of the World

Things to do and see

- Have fun on the Ski Tracks.
- Ride the Cable Cars.
- Try a Snowmobile Ride.
- Visit the Hot Pool.

The Top of the World is the place for winter sports.

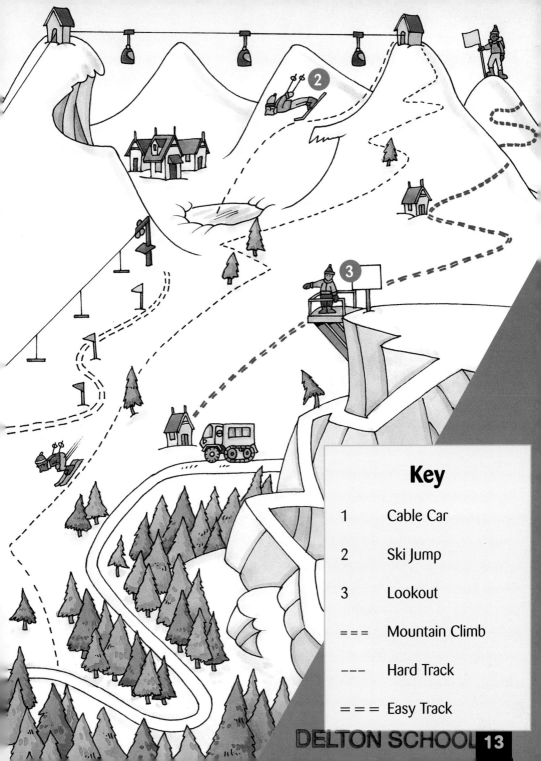

Key

1	Cable Car
2	Ski Jump
3	Lookout
= = =	Mountain Climb
- - -	Hard Track
= = =	Easy Track

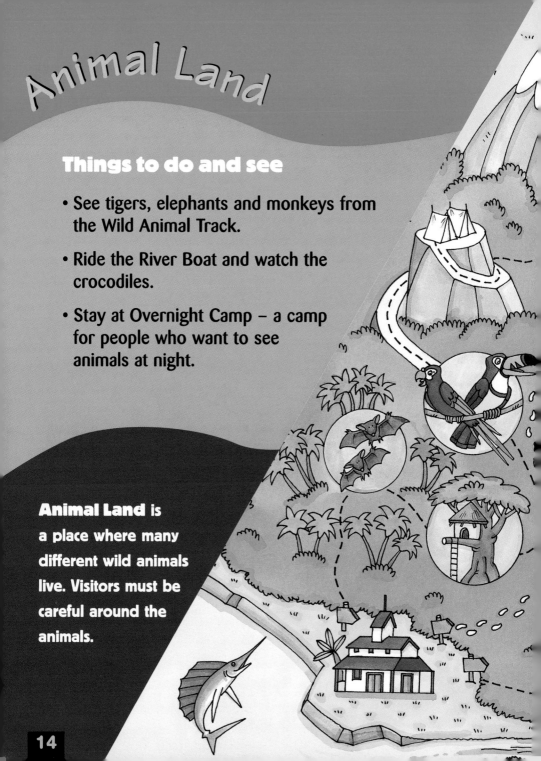

Animal Land

Things to do and see

- See tigers, elephants and monkeys from the Wild Animal Track.

- Ride the River Boat and watch the crocodiles.

- Stay at Overnight Camp – a camp for people who want to see animals at night.

Animal Land is a place where many different wild animals live. Visitors must be careful around the animals.

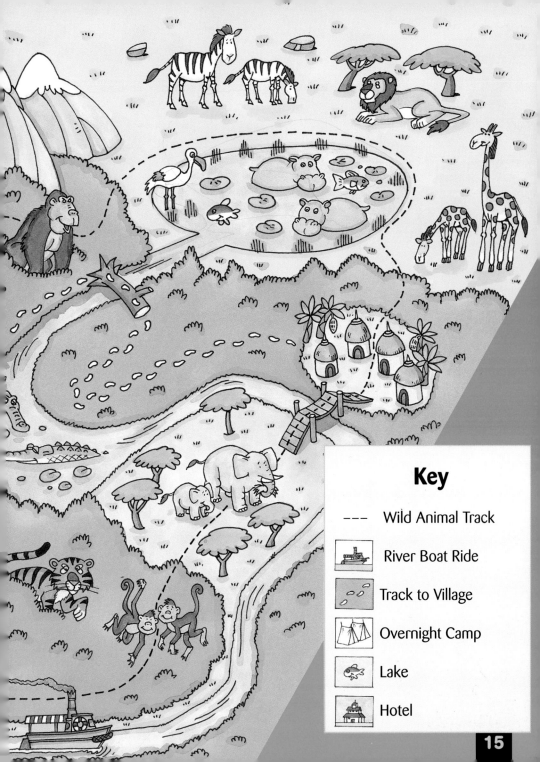

Key

--- Wild Animal Track

River Boat Ride

Track to Village

Overnight Camp

Lake

Hotel

Fun Zone

Highlights

The Billionaire Island traps catch many visitors.

Parrot Pool at Parrot Land

Dinosaurs in Dinosaur Land

The pools in the World of the Future

The Snowmobile Ride at The Top of the World

The River Boat Ride in Animal Land

What is a travel guide?

A travel guide gives information about:

• places to visit

• things to do and see

How to Write a Travel Guide

Step One

Make a map about a place to visit.

A map can have:
- signs
- symbols
- colour coding
- labels
- compass

Key

1	Lookouts
2	Talk School
3	Egg Nursery
4	Parrot Pools
5	Parrot Play Centre
----	Walking Track

Step Two

Make a key for your map.

Step Three

Use the map to write some information.

List some things to do.

List some things to see.

Things to do and see

- Visit the Parrot Pools –
  where parrots play
  on hot days.
- Visit the Parrot Play Centre
  – where young parrots
  have some fun.
- Visit "Talk School" –
  where parrots learn to
  talk.

19

Guide Notes

Title: **Fun Zone**
Stage: Launching Fluency

Text Form: Travel Guide – Maps
Approach: Guided Reading
Processes: Thinking Critically, Exploring Language, Processing Information
Written and Visual Focus: Maps, Key

THINKING CRITICALLY
(sample questions)
- Why do you think people would like to visit Fun Zone?
- If you were visiting the World of the Future, what things would you find the most exciting and why?
- If you were an old person, what activity would you like best and why?
- What do you think you would see from the lookout track on Billionaire Island?

EXPLORING LANGUAGE

Terminology
Spread, author and illustrator credits, ISBN number

Vocabulary
Clarify: zone, future, snowmobile, billionaire, buggy, highlights, monorail
Nouns: park, parrot, people, balloon
Verbs: live, ride, watch
Singular/plural: buggy/buggies, volcano/volcanoes, person/people

Print Conventions
Colon, dash, inverted commas: ("Talk School")

Phonological Patterns
Focus on short and long vowel **o** (z**o**ne, din**o**saur, r**o**b**o**t, h**o**t, t**o**p)
Discuss base words – exciting, buggies
Look at suffix **ful** (care**ful**)